CALLS FOR HELP

CALLS FOR HELP

Greg T. Miraglia

atmosphere press

For
The Girl in the Flammable Skirt
&
Dionysus
&
Thank you, Dan

I am – I should be held together by –

but I am breaking up...

-John Berryman, from "Op. Posth. No. 8"

1
We all fall down

You keep green,
even after you fell.
I keep green, to keep level.
It cared me like that
like Ophelia off the stairs,
and flexed a muscle of scares.

Dion: Alex had a few extra hands
when that walk turned into a crash
my hands were elsewhere.
She needs to take it in bits,
not roping back at excess.
Some of the hands around her
are grabbing more than giving.

I stay quiet,
you are too nice.
You stay as, and stay level
don't let those hands push,
you've already been down the stairs,
be aware some of us care.

2
Windfall

You let them
unquestionably alter you.
Choices stain us – I
want to live with your stains.
My fabric is far from clean
it's still together.

Dion: She is a force that can erase
worry, even when one should.
She can make a heart swell,
while giving it no quarter.
Her gale keeps him on his feet
or passes undetected.

It is our few moments
that remind me,
that I have fallen into the wind.
You make me wonder
does the wind care?

3
Laying on her Bed

You let me,
sometime I'd like to hear
you say, no.
The smell of your coat
is more green, than red.

Dion: She would not appreciate
the portrait framed from her
everyday tasks:
Sowing her yoga pants,
painting her nails,
sitting cross-legged at the computer,
highlighting, and writing.

If you find my presence distracting,
tell me to leave.
Your presence is a source of calm for me,
filling any emptiness
that might leave me restless.
I can't be
a person, pillow or puppet?

Call #4

I don't stand in lines,
you divide them all as you choose,
I will between them,
in between sides,
underwriting
aggressive competition.

Dion: He notices all the bodies as every body
builds on the burden of his mind.
She connects with lines.
Ink sweats at his forced impartiality,
words fall off his epidermis
from where each letter was placed.
She can hold focus
as he holds indecision,
every letter from his brain
melts off his arm
as he tries to ignore them.

You stand in lines,
I truly wish I could
stand with you.
On your side,
underwriting
aggressive pacifism.

5

To be an Accomplice

Might as well fucking stab me;
this double-edge dagger
highlights my desire.
Did Astrophil feel blessed
to see Stella's smile?

Dion: She regards relationships
as jello,
neither solid nor liquid,
just absolutely mundane
wobbling and green.

Seriously, just let me
fucking care about you.
Supernova's argue within my chest,
and only you can sing them to sleep.

Call #6

If I am libido machine,
biochemical model,
I cannot judge.
Can I actually la... care?

Dion: He is pissed off at the margins,
and the margin creators.
Every person needs vetted,
temporary, long term, friend,
acquaintance, douchebag.
She makes him happy
and he argues internally.
The argument doesn't matter,
he's man,
descendant of damned
margin creators.

Tear away my skin,
rip off my balls,
if they prevent growth
I don't need them.

7
Silent Meal

You have to appreciate the air
how it just stays there,
Eating in it, breathing in it.
All this soy sauce and rice
is drowning,
dinner has a way of be –
ing downing.

Dion: He picks at his food between looks around.
The rice and pasta soak helplessly.
Headphones are the final wall
between him and the outside world.
In this case, it's the side of care,
he terms, 'pointless wanting.'

I'm not sure this food had a chance,
I wasn't going to give it a chance.
Eating this, tasting it,
bland came along and I wanted sharp
tasting eats,
personality in the food – it's not just the body
that's sweet.

Call #8

"I can see the weight," said Dion.
It is pointless wanting, the want goes on.
I am old like moldy bread,
and he reminds me that he and Alex are not.
Some great matter.
Society has names for me.

Dion: I am far from physically acrobatic,
my summersaults are intellectual,
like my namesake my issues are excess.
I am his only tie to reachout.
Alex does not reachout to him,
others do not reachout to him,
the godly arcana serpent of wine, does.

"I am tired of the wait," said Dion.
"So heavy, I am too," I answered on.
It turns out we never ordered,
I, too lackadaisical, Dion, too inquisitive,
must be some great matter,
such as cradle-robbing.

Call #9

This is not about you,
who am I kidding? It is about you.
You're like this soup,
these beans in this broth
won't say, no, if I try to eat it,
not saying no, isn't a yes.

Dion: Alex made up her mind,
she also left room for it to be changed.
He doesn't need consent from bean soup,
however, he wants consent from Alex.
He wanted to be with her long enough
for things to crash and burn.
If he was soup,
it would look like an advert
and taste like the paper it was printed on.
They've known each other for months
and she hasn't noticed
that he's fucked up –
or hasn't said anything.

Why do I feel this for you?
Fuck-it there's nothing I can do.
You're like this soup,
I want to wrap it up and take it home,
something's stopping me, like this place,
everything is stopping me, like you, Alex.

10
Alex:

I had a dream
that I fell down the stairs again.
It was as it seemed,
a bruised memory,
a concussed figment.
I'm grateful the sun caught me
with friends.

Dion: She felt the quiet of the dark room,
then she got out of bed
and cleaned the quiet.
She heard the world outside,
she missed the sky.
Feeling her recycled coat,
she sniffed it, briefly before
hanging it up.

It felt like a dream
when it first happened.
It was not as it seemed,
a confused memory,
a robust figment,
however, I still got to see the sky
in the end.

11
At His Worst

I was energy yesterday
like an infinite ping-pong match,
I had an unmatched hunger
like a bear before hibernation.
The more my tongue begged
the more,
the more,
with sleeplessness,
no lining without silver.

He hides it goodish.
Three lines of thought ran
through his mind, simultaneously.
Until they didn't.
Until thoughts were seldom.
Open as a jar, sometimes he overflows
and other times he begs
for the heavy lid to be lifted.
He's used to hiding
from the world's super-citizens,
and mental-health amateurs.

Today concrete shoes hold me down,
a heavy sole sits on my chest,
today my appetite ran off
with kinetic sputterings and tastebuds,
today my eyelids are boulders
and I could doze any furniture.

12
Complimentary

Let me rescind that dagger,
in its doubling down glory,
like Berryman rescinded Henry's deaths.
Stella was a bad comparison,
this is not her story.
It's not even yours.

He is jello, or pudding,
Alex doesn't need consent.
She has to take the opportunity
that escapes him.
Sometimes he wants to click the undo-button;
this is not online Go versus the computer.
Its versus the cup, or spoon.

Fuck it. I'm wide open,
double divided in obsess-sin,
re-inventing my form, for you.
I shouldn't say that. For them.
This story is not for Rosaline.
It's not even for you.

13
Their Good Flaws

Patchy human-Dalmatian,
charmingly distant,
dancey animation,
smiley resistance.

She lives on waves of Mraz,
she's a Marley model of Bohemia,
center of social congregation,
she's 'come on Eileen,' giddy,
arm spinning smoke dragon.
He lives on waves of Cohen,
he's heart-driven neo-beatnik,
island of social dysfunction,
he's 'let's get to the point,' chill,
walk in the park drink fountain.

Sketchy human-kaleidoscope,
charmingly near,
tragedy full hope,
commonly sincere.

14
Stage Work

I can write a script.

All the levers and pullies
of the back stage,
her chaotic 'home sweet…'
'there's no place like…'
'if he only had a…'
He had a home there once,
not like Alex has now.

Alex: Not sure I need a man,
"Need is not necessarily the point…"
Need is a limitation, a cage
"… This will have no effect on the stage."
So you say.

Call #15

You work traffic,
wish I spent traffic.
You're a theatrical architect
or you will be.
I need to work your traffic,
my traffic is slow.

He feels his mind slowing at the edges,
her edges are fast.
He has words accumulated,
more than her actions done.
Volumes of jello.

Friction can't stop you,
you careen, you do.
I'm a poetic architect
or I will be.
I need to uncorrugate my traffic,
let you be my recourse.

16
Still as the North Star

You make me Ahab,
mutiny my focus, sometimes,
but there is no white whale,
only the vessel.
You anchor me. Hold me still
in the waves.

She worries.
He doesn't wish to be one.
They are not together.
He floats away as the light goes.
She doesn't throw a line.
I'm a romantic,
if it were up to me
they'd be together.
They are equally rocking.

I want to be capsized one day
to spare me from this chase,
you allow my focus solidarity.
There is no other course
I would follow,
you hold me still, as the sky
holds the north star.

17
Level Ground

An image pedestalled
is a grave disrespect, in these times.
I will not cast conjecture on your image.
My academic equals are worms
and my meaning was lost.

A blue couch can be a paralytic,
he cannot see her as a state of meditation,
as dishonourable as being called a goddess,
high-born appreciation, in these days,
is given to the pointlessly-wealthy
and porn-star crowds.

Your image held up
would forget your kindness,
too entrancing a smile.
The insults conjured through
such mistakes, are too grim,
a worm such as I, only sees pedestals.

18
Excuse the Heart

What if you're the one
that forces my dog-heart
to betray everything it knows
to chase only the?
What if I leave
and crows litter my path?

He's pushed by want.
He's pulled by respect.
He's there phasing in and out.
Her legs dance in the moment,
she talks hot as boiling oil under eggs.
He can feel the oil pop up and sting his ego.
He'd give anything to feast and howl.

What if you're the soul
and all others refuse my dog-heart?
What if my dog-heart refuses them,
leaving me there again
in crow-covered abandonment,
my losses littering the?

19
The Day

I voted proudly for Obama,
then I cowardly didn't vote,
then I voted in the primaries,
then I voted for a woman.

All that he remembers after that
is insults
emanating from an Orange Hair
Microphone.
The microphone had white hair
a month into office.
After the election, he got drunk,
and Alex got high.

I hid proudly in my room,
then I cowardly hid again,
then I hid in many good causes,
then I came out of hiding.

20
Water Falls

I couldn't imagine being moth-mouthed,
if only orange mics and red elephants were.
My last tears were for North Dakota,
our drinking water might change, not the soda.
Damn, did anybody pay attention to Oroville?
I need to muster the talking-type will.

He will not leave.
Alex will leave.
He watches his government
chase away its citizens.
Trudeau is a nice alternative.
He goes down with the ship.
She has no qualms about spending
four years elsewhere.
He can't afford that.

I couldn't imagine being forced out,
to abandon our Seneca Fall's heroines.
We never more needed checks and Judiciary,
signs and pickets never more necessary.
They push forward a faucet flowing black,
if you leave, for your health, don't come...

Call #21

I saw this sign
"No Food Outside," wasted food,
their establishment wastes my time,
while some starve in stomach, I in mind.
They waste oil and energy to fry.
They waste paying employees to waste.

He sees this sign as an affront,
as if they declared building a wall
to keep food IN (the trash).
He believes in storing leftovers,
he believes in honouring a cook's hardwork.
Food was liberated.

We were fucking stars,
but these celestial bodies deserve to starve?

22
Star Bright

I would so badly like to haunt
someone tonight, if ever so charmingly,
to compliment the glowing light,
whether or not it is my right.
Never have I seen a cascading tail
like this blonde one.

She is a maverick star ascending,
each molecule broke down
and reformed, Alex.
He might be a dwarf star,
but I am no astronomer, to know.
You, the reader heard me, the narrator;
She, he, and I are no astronomers,
although we were once stars,
except her.

I worry my presence serves to daunt,
when I wish to be disarming,
to edify your description,
and maybe allow for re-scription.
Your illustration is that sky map
that is partial to your mass known.

23
North Words

It feels like garbage,
consistent spewing of words,
some have been ravaged,
they can't be good.
This is my Ishmael's whale definitions,
and my Hemingway's life.

Inspiration is not an excuse
for derivatives, so he thinks.
He wonders if Alex secretly hates him,
like he secretly hates his writing
that appears after long stretches of inspiration.
It comes and overstays its welcome.
He sees that.

A course correction
words due skyward in the North
with desire at its cross-section;
I should avoid inspiration,
or befall harpoons
and tough-guy personas.

24
Prevailing

I want to be hated like Frost
and Shakespeare in high school English.
The closest thing to a defunct God,
I can only stand two destinations:
An English burden
or Alex supporter.

He has called her a reward, she is not,
but he knows she is the standard,
he cannot prevail unless
he has like her, careening traffic.
Alex's standard will move him
closer to defunct-God-status,
without her traffic
his destinations are only standing.

I want you to be hated in every
elementary directorial course,
be known like Stanislavski and Welles.
Stand in your highest direction
through your enduring traffic.

25
The Difference Between Stars

You were stardust last,
I've had a greater living past
stuck here in bodily form
to find you later, confounding.
I've been acetylene burning fast
through the common and intimate.

He's young for grey hair,
but he found one.
Alex was far from grey,
only nineteen years
out of the universe's bosom.
He saw her glow
as if she was still a star.
He noticed his dim light
and looked closer to his final poof!

My particles must have broken down,
while yours kept whooshing 'round.
No longer meteors or stars,
and I am still breaking, ever faster.
No longer am I burning hydrogen.

26
Thievery

Is it 'alright, alright, alright?'
I'm taking you and them and all
in my work.
You've laughed and smiled and blushed
at my work.
Have I stolen you?
Have I twisted your fact?

The administration filled him
with fear, that he might create
alternative perceptions and fake facts.
He stole Lit. cult, pop cult, classic cult,
his greatest sin is stealing her.
Was theft his only skill?
He didn't trade inside like Price,
or embezzle thoughts like Manafort's money.
He traded outside with open transactions.
She knew he was stealing.

Is it 'cool, cool, cool'
that my treasure trove or tree
of knowledge
is full of, all old, unoriginal stolen
my knowledge?
Please catch me
before I run off with your fact.

Call #27

Let me care for the both of us
enough for forks to be forks
and spoons to be spoons
and not enough for supper.
Not enough to let you suffer.

Once everything is in place
he needs to eat,
What's next,
if the tables set and no one arrives?
The scheduling was her deficiency,
never committing to a time.
He mixes forks and spoons,
left or right side of the plate?
She mixes minutes and hours,
right or wrong side of commitment.

Let's be as we are
and let go of concerns;
left, wrong, or right.
Let our hearts be eaten together
by the morning's blue light.

28
Yielding

You ebb and flow,
owing nothing when you go.
I fair in the ebb
and try not to feel owed.
Your ebb holds me close,
your flow not so.

She would have a talent
if it wasn't a defense mechanism.
Just once more, so he thinks.
It's never once more,
that stop-sign phrase
is the yellow-light of the psyche.
We all speed on through,
until she chooses to give him
a red-light.

Alex: You stay and go,
owing nothing off your flow.
I fair when you stay
and forcefully try to know
you have nothing owed,
and I, nothing gained so.

Call #29

I remember when loneliness
was not synonymous with languishing.
Prospectives were barren,
rather than unrequited.
Lucrative populations now leave me
tunneled with horse-blinders.

I try, for your sake, to shake off these blinders,
my track is cyclical:
Solitude melts into languishing
answered unrequited
or half-stunted in dirty sheets,
drink, drink, solitude.

30
Behind Personae

It bursts, flowing outward,
joy folds in on fear.
"I wanted my first impression
to be our first impression."
I contain this,
blinking incessantly
like a broken fire alarm.

His aspirations are ant hills.
He sees mountains,
a climb that begins
and ends with her.
Her climb may include him,
although it is not readily apparent.
They have indecision in common.

My soul feels it, outward,
fear folds back in on joy.
"Realism defined impressions
through lenses of obsession."
You contain this,
hiding consistently
like a turtle in a shell.

31
Horn Section

You have me like a horn section,
a well-placed clarinet,
or perfect trumpet.
You make me listen,
your sound makes me stay.

Jazz and Soul knows how it effects,
so does she.
All he can do is sit in the audience/
step into her playing,
he knows how he wants her to feel,
he just doesn't know how to play.

I want to be your horn section,
a well-set saxophone,
or tireless trombone,
so you might want to listen,
so you might want to stay.

32
To Need Reciprocation

I want and yearn
my yearning may turn
my image of you,
and I cannot allow my want
to change my view.

He would give anything
just to enjoy the heat
from her sunlight,
rather than be burned
by her gaze.

I'd like you to return
or leave me to yearn
by lying or telling the truth
to break my spirit,
and deprive me of your rays.

Us on Earth

'Bino, J. Cole, and Lamar
keep me warm,
instead of cold Lit. white.
Tie me to a universal write.

His green choices are for you,
for all living things, for all Earth.
Those who wrote our past
attacked the globe and themselves.
His winters have been too warm
less real than Winter once was.

I will not define myself
through skin and sex,
my planet is not only
dirt and spherical.
We are more, empirically.

34
Cardiac Fusion

I wish a blizzard on my heart,
however, the burning fusion
you sparked within
prevents such defense,
stops the glacier formin'.

She cleared the fog for him,
his heart's foremen
resist management's requests.
It pains him to be less persistent,
it burns for her,
it tires from burning,
it continues in exhaustion,
it desires to continue,
it fractures in desire.
Unclouded he moves toward her,
he knew he could only follow,
she lets him follow
without asking him.

You lead me. I ask for it.
No qualm with my delusion?
I found within
less despair, a need to care.
Please, blizzard begin.

35
Push Me Away

Tell me to leave,
tell me to chew dust,
tell me to track off the icy pier,
tell me to bob for whales,
tell me to dig to Guam,
tell me to helter-skelter into old ruins.

Either way he will be in a bottle,
the return portion of care
is never the right amount.
His pillow smells of gin, at night.
Her coat smells of mj, at night.
He hides in solitude, in the day.
She hides behind smiles, in the day.
Either way if she keeps moving
the boredom won't remind her
about the cracks in her image.

Tell me to go,
tell me to take a climb,
tell me to go jump off a volcano,
tell me to wander the woods,
tell me to find the road's end,
tell me to soul search until I find another.

36
Gravitational Conclusions

I twist the stairs,
what choice do I have?
I've seen them go straight up,
even them go straight down,
I twist, although I thought
about going straight down.

She found dysfunction normal,
his down would change her,
he didn't think so.
His country was governed that way,
why couldn't he down?

You fell stairs.
Knowing all result,
my down would be
purposeful and harder.
No sun would find me caught.
My dysfunction must be derivative.

37
Talisman

I have the stone flat and smooth
with one dimple at its end,
that was picked up by you
and given to me, a new friend.
I still carry it whole
to keep still my heart and hole.

He's foolish to believe in this magic,
his voodoo for her by her,
his promise that there's time.
Her gift, chosen from that stony
beach, on a day that ended
in his defeated heart
by her solitary stand,
only after the guiding of his hand.
She fatally wounded his hope
with that shard of sedimentary.

Your dimpled stone is faith's possibility,
the grey of freedom, rather than melancholy,
its presence acts as your lips when smiley
and allows my mind to cast down folly.
I might lose this, and when I do,
it may mean I will forever lose you.

38

Timing

Alex: Misfortune happens every day,
this feeling is unfamiliar as parched lips,
I've drank water for so long,
thirst a week away,
he is water of recent days.

She is as foolish as he is.
They wallow in soul light,
alright it feels new to her,
maybe new like the distance of old,
not new like unseen lands,
or unknown pleasures.
His week was of withdrawal,
knowing every second of her
was a day's ecstasy.
She finally and foolishly felt as he did.
He finally and foolishly felt
he had to leave her,
end his haunting persistence.

Alex: Dry lips beg for condensation
and there's a feeling this thirst will last
like he's not coming back,
because of my continuous alienation
throughout his continual articulation.

39
Misplaced

Alex: The feng shui is incomplete
like something needs to be here,
my pillows are not enough,
everything wouldn't be the right stuff.
You once laid your head here.
You were my shadow's tail.

She couldn't shift her bed
or move her desk.
It used to be fine.
She reorganized her closet,
re-alphabetized her book shelf,
straighten the knickknacks on her desk,
swept, dusted,
re-swept, re-dusted.
Her room was unacceptable.
She left to get green.
He *could not* move on.
He *could* walk away.

Alex: You reverse My Fair Lady'd me,
I've grown accustom to your being.
I told you not to wait, you opted not,
and you waited like at a bus-stop
for a bus that wasn't seeing
you on the schedule, now it does.

40
Daylight's Drawbacks

I have to produce,
cannot fall into thoughts of her,
cannot slide down to my true content.
She must be the reward for me
that I wish to be for her.

He's a piece of shit,
writing him is tiresome.
She's incomplete,
only desiring to drown.
They are both garbage.
Nobody is as certain or pacifying as her.
Nobody is as conflicted or loyal as him.
Maybe there is, but I change my mind,
this pair of independent freaks
shouldn't ever end up together.

Alex: I must moderate,
cannot hide in excess,
cannot allow cracks to push him away.
He must be the net
that I wish to be for him.

Call #41

I am used to mosquitos,
maybe I am one,
and my actions are sucking
dry you and your joy.

There were days he darkened her eyes,
but not every shade was his effect.
If she numbered his weight,
it would be less than most
she's known.
They shouldn't have even talked.

Why do they suck at me?
I must suck at them,
or all, or you, or it,
dry life and its joy.

Call #42

She hasn't been given enough time.
Her isolation matters,
however hers can be fulfilled.
What are we thinking?
Sexism, misogyny, feminism,
biases, prejudices, loyalties
to parties or ethnicities?
Ugly words, a divisive herd,
and here I am drowning,
as he drowns,
as she drowns.

43
In the Distance

Alex: His being there was brief
like a passing cloud
just blew by.

She was his cloud for so long,
passed without point.
She's too late and deserves her end.
He's too early and deserves
his tearing length.
He passed at such great distance
that his cloud was only noticed by her.
She could only notice.

Alex: Could I reach?
Arms stretched out
only reminds me he's away.

44
Quarantined

Alex: If he was here:
his tongue falls heavier than hers,
his hands touch lighter,
but she hesitates less.
I can't continue, I confess.

Sex was needed when it was needed,
but she never needed feelings.
Alex saw him in her,
she saw him in stands and fantasies.
She now hesitated
which never halted his replacements.
Instead of two rays of light,
she felt radiated upon.

Alex: He is not here,
only this woman's heavy touch,
even the last guy
was too hot and too cold.
Where's just right, familiar, old?

45
Tradeoffs

My coat smells of green,
it's lost like my place,
the mirror reveals cracks in my face.
These seem less born and more
hand-me-downed from her falling star.
I was whole once.

Molecules both starred
and wet could not help.
My mind everchanging,
wishes it could help.
Reborn and they still don't fly
as the others do.
They forget each other
until the other passes.

Alex: My pillow smells of gin,
it's misplaced, traded, missing.
I never *needed* before as irritating as a fly,
more cat than ever,
empty for his dog-hearted snuggles.
These cracks were glued once.

Call # 46

"You had to renege,
she was not returning
your affections," Dion said.
I had no rebuttal,
only the trappings
of emotion, frilly and annoying.

His talisman flares
in its pocket.
It's voice miles from us.
Down he feels.
Down, he holds.
Drinks and green
could not contain
his displaced muscle.

I poured another glass of wine.
"Frankly, haven't you
had enough?" Dion asked.
I could not recoil, only bask.
It tampers temporarily,
the frilly.

About Atmosphere Press

Atmosphere Press is an independent, full-service publisher for excellent books in all genres and for all audiences. Learn more about what we do at atmospherepress.com.

We encourage you to check out some of Atmosphere's latest releases, which are available at Amazon.com and via order from your local bookstore:

The Unordering of Days, poetry by Jessica Palmer

It's Not About You, poetry by Daniel Casey

A Dream of Wide Water, poetry by Sharon Whitehill

Radical Dances of the Ferocious Kind, poetry by Tina Tru

The Woods Hold Us, poetry by Makani Speier-Brito

My Cemetery Friends: A Garden of Encounters at Mount Saint Mary in Queens, New York, nonfiction and poetry by Vincent J. Tomeo

Report from the Sea of Moisture, poetry by Stuart Jay Silverman

The Enemy of Everything, poetry by Michael Jones

The Stargazers, poetry by James McKee

The Pretend Life, poetry by Michelle Brooks

About the Author

Greg T. Miraglia is a graduate of Wells College where he received their Class of 1905 Poetry Prize. His poetry has been in the Garbanzo Literary Journal, Aerogram, and in Cowboy Poetry Press. His poems have been presented at the 2015 Bridgewater Inter-national Poetry Festival and been part of the 2016 Nevermore METRO Immersive Arts Festival. Greg also writes short fiction and nonfiction essays. He is a proud member of the WriteOn Writers group. Read more from Greg at GregThePoet.com